ASK Leading Women™

MAKE THE MOST

OF MENTORING

Capitalize on Mentoring
and Take Your Career
to the Next Level

SUSAN L. COLANTUONO
CEO and Founder, Leading Women

For information on reprints and/or bulk orders, contact:
Interlude Productions
PO Box 1124
Charlestown, RI 02813
USA
+1-401-789-0441

Printed in the United States of America
14 13 12 11 10   5 4 3 2 1

Library of Congress Cataloging-in-Publication Data

Colantuono, Susan Lee
    Make the Most of Mentoring: Capitalize on Mentoring and Take Your Career
to the Next Level/ Susan L. Colantuono
        p. cm.
ISBN 978-0-9673129-3-4
1. Mentoring in business—Handbooks, manuals, etc. 2. Career development
3. Women executives 4. Leadership in women 4. Management I. Colantuono,
Susan Lee II. Title III. Capitalize on Mentoring and Take Your Career to the
Next Level

HF5385.C65 2012

All *ASK Leading Women*™ books offer inspiring and
practical solutions for women as they move from
career-start to the C-suite and onto corporate boards.

When you *ASK Leading Women,* you get cutting-edge content,
ready-to-apply tools, insights from self-assessments, and examples
from successful women who act as your virtual mentors.

Other Books by Susan Colantuono

*No Ceiling, No Walls: What women haven't been told about
leadership from career-start to the corporate boardroom*

Build Your Career: Getting Ahead Without Getting Out

Make Room for JOY: Finding Magical Moments in Your Everyday Life

With thanks to Dave Chichester and
Wendy Susco—my first mentors!

Table of Contents

Why Mentoring Isn't Getting You Where You Want to Go

Whether you began your career decades ago or just last year, you've probably heard that you need a mentor if you want to advance in your career. This advice has been given based on years of research into the important role that mentors play in the career success of executives. This same research has prompted organizations (perhaps even yours) to launch or sustain corporate mentoring programs.

If you've listened to and acted on the advice to get a mentor or to participate in your organization's mentoring program, you likely had a positive experience. However, it's probably equally likely that your experience didn't have the impact on your career that you hoped it would. And if you are responsible for a corporate mentoring program, you might well be disappointed with the minimal impact it's had on women's advancement.

These experiences raise the question, why isn't mentoring getting women where they want to go?

I believe the answer is that, for women, mentoring has been less than effective because of how we think about mentoring, the way our thinking influences the structure of corporate mentoring programs and the way it's shaped the mentoring interactions that most women have. In fact, conventional wisdom about mentoring totally ignores the one skill area women most often lack but most often need in order to advance their careers—what I call The Missing 33%™. Because of this gap, current paradigms about mentoring seriously underserve women and corporate mentoring programs fall short of their goals.

Over the past few years, through several significant experiences as well as my work with women leaders, I've come to the conclusion that the ways we think about and engage in mentoring are flawed, as are the ways we design and implement mentoring programs. (And I can say this with some authority, as I designed corporate mentoring programs in the past.) Ever since I reframed *my* understanding of mentoring, I've been sharing these insights with women across the U.S. and around the globe. Learning to think about mentoring in a new way has helped hundreds of women—and making this shift will be important to you as well.

I've written *Make the Most of Mentoring* to help you shift your thinking whether you are a:

- Woman who wants to grow in her career,
- Man or woman who mentors women or
- Professional who designs and/or manages corporate mentoring programs.

If you fall into any of these categories, *Make the Most of Mentoring* offers you a profoundly different—and immeasurably more impact-ful—understanding of mentoring. And, on a practical note, it also offers dozens of concrete tips for being a better protégé or mentor and for enhancing your corporate mentoring program.

What you won't find in this book is advice to get a mentor, why it's important to have a mentor or the protocols of a mentoring rela-tionship. This information is amply covered in other books, on the internet and in the materials that accompany most formal mentoring programs. And we at Leading Women cover key information about the protocol of mentoring relationships in our online Be a Mentor/ Find a Mentor resources *(www.LeadingWomen.biz)*.

When *Providence Business News* named me Ally and Mentor for Business Women, I was deeply honored. At the same time I felt compelled to reach beyond my network to mentor other women whose goals are to build flourishing careers. This book is my way of reaching out to help you make the most of mentoring—as a protégé, mentor or person responsible for a corporate program. I sincerely hope that you find it a valuable resource.

How to Make the Most of This Book

To help you get the greatest return from your time spent reading this book, I strongly encourage you to read it in the order the material is presented:

- **Part I** explains why it's essential to rethink mentoring.
- **Part II** serves up a new recipe for mentoring success.
- **Part III** is chock full of tips for making the most of mentoring—tips for protégés, mentors and professionals who are responsible for corporate mentoring programs.

If you're like me, you may be tempted to go right to the tips in Part III. However, to truly capitalize on these tips, you must first shift your thinking about mentoring. That's why Parts I and II offer a pointed analysis of why we think about mentoring as we do and why we must think about it differently. (And, quite frankly, the tips won't make much sense without having read Parts I and II.)

In addition to the information about mentoring presented in this book, I've posted a number of **free resources** on my website to help you fully leverage your mentoring relationships and corporate mentoring program. Whenever you see this symbol (▶) throughout the book, it is an indication that you can go to *www.MaketheMostofMentoring.com* to find a free resource related to the information.

One last note: Please indulge me in a brief comment on language. As an English major, I prefer the more classic word *protégé* to the more recently coined[1] word *mentee* to describe "one who benefits from a mentor."

Now, let's prepare for a mind shift that will help you Make the Most of Mentoring.

PART ONE

Why We Need to Rethink Mentoring

"Some people just wait for someone to take them under their wings, but they should just find someone's wings to grab onto. Gaining a mentor is up to you."
—ANDREA JUNG, CEO
AVON

"Let mentors find you. If you ask someone to be your mentor and they agree, then they probably aren't going to push you as hard as someone who is grooming you for the next level."
—INDRA NOOYI, CEO
PEPSICO

Conventional Wisdom About Mentoring

If the quotes on the previous page seem contradictory to you, don't be surprised. While much current advice about mentoring is valuable, much is also contradictory, confusing and at times unhelpful. In part this is because conventional wisdom about mentoring hasn't changed much since the 1980s when I first started to help companies design and launch corporate mentoring programs.

Conventional wisdom about mentoring can be summed up as:
- Mentors make a difference in a career.
- Successful men have mentors.
- Women need mentors to get ahead.
- Mentors are trusted confidantes who give you confidence, help you develop skills and guide the steps you take in your career.

To understand why these are today's core beliefs about mentoring, there are 5 things you need to know about the history of mentoring.

1. Mentoring is Rooted in the Dawn of Time
For all of human history, women and men have prepared girls and boys for their roles in society. They've done this informally through stories, role modeling, teaching, advising and rewards and punishments.

The use of the word *mentor* to describe this informal activity has its roots in the ancient Greek story of Odysseus who, as he sailed off to fight the Trojan wars, left his son Telemachus under the care of his friend Mentor. Since then, the word *mentor* has come to mean:

1. A wise and trusted counselor or teacher.
2. An influential senior sponsor or supporter.[2]
3. Someone who imparts wisdom to and shares knowledge with a less experienced colleague.

When you read the word *mentor* in this book these are the definitions behind it.

2. Modern-Day Mentoring Evolved as an Organizational Tool

Informal mentoring has been an important fixture in organizations. It probably has its roots in the practice of craftsmen taking on apprentices, but we certainly know that it has been a part of industrial organizations. Why has mentoring been so important in organizations?

Mentoring arose as an organization's informal solution to the need for future leadership. Think of it as an informal process for succession planning. That's why for centuries, senior men used informal mentoring to groom more junior men to replace them—in other words to fill future supervisory, management or executive vacancies.

Junior employees **were groomed to make a contribution to the organization at higher levels;** they were *not* individually groomed for career success. This is a subtle and important distinction. Mentoring might help the individual, but evolved to serve the system.

3. Women Were Left Out of Mentoring Experiences

The relationship between having a mentor and advancing in a career was first noted in the mid- to late 1970s when research found that successful men reported having had mentors (see #2 above). This was the same time that women began entering the workforce with the expectation of building careers.

Unfortunately, because nearly all of the people in positions to recognize the need for and groom successors were men, most women were left out. This created fertile ground for action.

4. Corporate Mentoring Programs Proliferate in the 1980s

Capitalizing on this fertile ground, progressive organizations created *formal* mentoring programs as one tool to help women (and other underrepresented groups) advance. The phrase *mentoring program* first appeared in widespread usage in the early 1980s. Thirty years later, the World Economic Forum reported that 59% of the companies it surveyed had formal mentoring and networking programs.

5. Mentoring Program Designers Weren't Informally Mentored

Your organization might have a formal mentoring program, and unless you work for one of the exceptional companies with women proportionately represented at all levels of management, you might look around and ask this question, *"If we have such a progressive corporate mentoring program, why are there still so few of us at the top?"*

Part of the reason is in the design of the program. Many of the professionals (including myself) who were tasked with designing formal mentoring programs were never informally mentored with the goal of grooming us for bigger contributions.

Although we might have had men encouraging our performance, we observed men's informal mentoring relationships from the outside and without a full understanding of the dynamics involved. To us, mentors looked like trusted confidantes whose role was to build confidence, help develop skills and guide the steps in a protégé's career. From our vantage point what we couldn't see was that **men advanced because of *what* they were mentored on, not simply because they had mentors.**

As a result much of the advice developed for corporate mentoring programs focuses on what designers could observe or surmise. This is why today there is:

- So much useful information available on the phases of mentoring, building a trusting relationship, the characteristics of a mentoring agreement, dos and don'ts of mentoring and the like. We *could* design a process for relationship building.
- So little written about *how* to use the mentoring relationship. We didn't know about The Missing 33%. We didn't understand what the protégé did to earn informal mentoring or the substance of the mentoring relationship— and so we *couldn't* give related advice.

If more of us had been informally mentored and able to see what was going on from the inside, three things would be different. There'd be a lot more useful information about capitalizing on mentoring relationships, we wouldn't need to differentiate mentors from sponsors and more women would be in more senior positions today.

Why Conventional Wisdom is Incomplete

The nature of mentoring today and the conventional wisdom about it leads to a serious problem: women are not being mentored on the one skill set they are most often lacking and most need to develop in order to advance—what I call The Missing 33%.

The Missing 33%
I first stumbled upon the importance of The Missing 33% during my research to help prepare women to take on leadership roles in organizations. It's described in detail in my book, *No Ceiling, No Walls: What women haven't been told about leadership from career-start to the corporate boardroom.*

If you haven't read *No Ceiling, No Walls*, here's a short summary:
- Advancement in organizations rests on a foundation of proven leadership skills. Here's how I define leadership: *"Leadership is using the greatness in you to achieve and sustain extraordinary outcomes by engaging the greatness in others."*
- The definition points to 3 interdependent components of leadership:
  1. **Use personal greatness** (e.g., attributes and strengths).
  2. **Achieve and sustain outcomes** (requiring business, strategic and financial acumen).

3. **Engage greatness in others** (e.g., interpersonal skills).
- Conventional wisdom about leadership over-focuses on 2 of the 3 components: interpersonal skills to engage others and attributes of personal greatness. That's in large part because these are areas where men need to improve. (Don't be offended. This isn't my opinion—I cite the research in *No Ceiling, No Walls*.) Over decades, studies have reported that women outshine men in these two components.
- The same studies report that managers rate men as outperforming women on 1 of the 3 components—achieve outcomes. **This is The Missing 33% of the leadership success equation for women. It is comprised of business, strategic and financial acumen.**

Disturbingly, our current research indicates that business, strategic and financial acumen account for 50% of the skills that executives seek in high potential candidates and that boards seek in C-suite executives.

A while ago I moderated a panel of men who are C-suite executives or senior managers. One of the questions I asked was what they look for in high potential candidates. They went on and on about looking for good interpersonal skills, someone who is trustworthy and ethical, a bias for action, an innovator, etc. Knowing that there was something they weren't saying, I asked, *"What about demonstrated business, strategic and financial acumen."* To a man, they replied, "That's a given."

Yet, even in Fortune 50 companies, leadership competency models and performance systems significantly under-emphasize these skills.
- Most leadership definitions, models and programs totally ignore or give only minimal attention to The Missing 33%.
- Most women aren't told about the importance of The Missing 33%.
- Most women aren't able to demonstrate business, strategic and financial acumen because they don't speak the Language of Power™ (which is the language of business).

This lack of emphasis is one key reason that women's advancement in organizations has slowed considerably in recent decades.

Whether you are an individual contributor, a senior manager or in between, you must address The Missing 33% to power up your leadership skills or you will be left behind. Sadly, in many organizations, the only way to get these skills is informally through mentoring. And while mentoring programs offer all kinds of advice about how to select a mentor, forming trusting relationships and creating a mentoring contract, many totally ignore the importance of using mentoring to build business, strategic and financial acumen. Because of this gap, conventional wisdom about mentoring seriously underserves women and corporate mentoring programs fall short of their goals.

How Corporate Mentoring Programs Fall Short

At face value, corporate mentoring programs work. Women and men who might not otherwise have access to them are able to enter mentoring relationships—often with people they'd not otherwise interact with. But this impact is a far cry from the expectation that mentoring programs will help women advance.

If the measure of the success of mentoring programs is significant advancement of women into senior positions, after more than 30 years the results have been disappointing. Since the 1980s, mentoring programs have helped women get to 50% representation in managerial and professional positions, but they haven't helped large numbers of women break into senior management or executive levels.

Why has such a promising solution fallen so short? To be fair, there are other dynamics that contribute to the uneven and glacially slow progress women have made, but that doesn't mean we shouldn't ask whether mentoring programs are all they could be. Because I've had a hand in creating today's reality, I've asked that question and identified 6 shortcomings. If you understand these 6 pitfalls, you'll be able to avoid them because you will have begun to rethink mentoring.

Pitfall # 1: Forced Matching

We know that before the 1980s, mentoring was informal and a mentor was a man with a vested interest in the development of a more junior colleague. With the advent of formal mentoring programs, forced matching became a central component.

Here's how mentoring works in most programs. Mentors volunteer to mentor because they believe they have something to offer, not because they are vested in the success of a particular protégé. Protégés are either hand selected or self-selected to participate.

Matches are made either through a manual process that assigns mentor/protégé pairs (or groups) or through an online process (kind of like online dating). As a result while the mentor may or may not have affinity for the protégé(s), the mentor rarely enters the relationship with the belief in the potential of the protégé to contribute at higher levels or in other parts of the organization.

In such forced matching situations, **mentors are rarely vested in the success of the protégé and are hesitant to invest social capital to advocate on her behalf**. This is why mentoring relationships are largely advisory, feedback or feel-good relationships. It's no wonder that so few protégés have been prepared to contribute at higher levels.

Please don't think that I'm suggesting that you shouldn't participate in your organization's formal mentoring program. Quite the contrary. A corporate mentoring program can be an incredibly valuable tool. As you'll find in Parts II and III, what I am suggesting is that to benefit from the promise of a corporate mentoring program, you must rethink what it is and how to use it.

Pitfall # 2: An Excessive Focus on Form and Process Rather Than Substance and Content

Today's mentoring programs are less successful than they could be because conventional wisdom, with its roots in the '70s, tells only half the story. Here's what I mean.

Let's assume that your company has matched you with a mentor and you want to make the most of the opportunity. You turn to the internet to search for advice about mentoring. You'll be confronted with millions of returns.

If you pick the first 20 most substantive articles (not written for entrepreneurs) and categorize them, you'll find that nearly all of them address one or both of the following topics:

1. Advice to get a mentor and why.
2. The protocol, phases or etiquette for a mentoring relationship.

You'll find an abundance of articles about executives who had mentors and the difference they made in their careers. You'll find advice about the phases of mentoring and the roles of the mentor and protégé in each phase. You'll read advice about seeking a mentor or waiting to be tapped as a protégé. You'll find examples of contracts to cement the expectations of the mentoring relationship. You'll learn about the importance of asking for and giving feedback. And on and on.

This over focus on form and process and lack of focus on substance and content (see Pitfall #4) is a tremendous disservice to women who want to advance.

Pitfall # 3: Gender Differences About Trust

Related to the focus on form and process is a frequent emphasis on the importance of giving and receiving feedback. That's why much of the guidance suggests that you have to create a deep trusting relationship. What no one tells you is that **what a *trusting relationship* means to most men is different than what it means to most women.** So here's what you have to know.

> *WARNING! What I'm reporting here is based on patterns discovered through research.[3] It doesn't imply that it's true for all men. Or that it's never true for women. I know many executive women who feel nearly the same about many of these points. And many men who believe differently about some.*

For women, trusting relationships are often built through shared life experiences (e.g., having children), discussing personal (and sometimes private) information, openness about our vulnerabilities and weakness and—I'm embarrassed to admit—shared complaints.

For most men, trust arises from loyalty—and loyalty arises from certain behaviors; behaviors based on the understanding that:

Personable ≠ Personal

Men tend to share personal information and vulnerability primarily with their wives, partners or lovers. Women primarily share personal information and vulnerability as a strategy to connect with anyone. If you try to build trust by sharing personal information or vulnerability with a male mentor, he might take you out of the category of competent businesswoman.

You Are Your Position

Probably because of experience playing sports, most men believe that the position you hold is what is critical to the business. They expect that the requirements of your position will always trump your personal preferences. For example, you might not enjoy detailed statistical analysis of monthly reports, but you do it because it's a key requirement of your position.

Loyalty means (and trust is built when) you live up to the responsibilities of your position, even when you don't like them. Women—even those who've played sports—don't always understand this and can appear disloyal by putting their personal perspectives ahead of the demands of the position.

There is a Code of Conduct for Disagreements

When it comes to building trust, your mentor will learn a lot about you based on how you handle disagreements. This is equally true for how you handle disagreements with him/her and how you portray the story of a disagreement with your boss (if you happen to share one). Most male mentors (and executives of both genders) expect that you will handle disagreements this way:

- State as fully and respectfully as you can your reasons for disagreement.

- Then accept and faithfully implement your boss's decision…even if it differs from your preference.
- Never complain in public about the decision.

Colin Powell, former Secretary of State and Chairman of the Joint Chiefs of Staff, illustrates this succinctly when he says,

> *"When we are debating an issue, loyalty means giving me your honest opinion, whether you think I'll like it or not. Disagreement, at this state, stimulates me. But once a decision is made, debate ends. From that point on, loyalty means executing the decision as if it were your own."*

Often women don't speak up, don't let go or will criticize publicly. These behaviors break the male code of conduct for disagreements in the Work World and can make women appear disloyal or untrustworthy.

You MUST Have His Back
In the final analysis, especially if your mentor is a man, trust depends on your mentor's belief that you will have his/her back. Anything your mentor says to you should never come back to embarrass him/her. How you follow through on agreements the two of you make will indicate whether or not you can be trusted.

And, even how you talk about your boss will indicate to your mentor whether or not you can be trusted to have your mentor's back. A complaint about your boss becomes a signal to your mentor that you aren't to be trusted.

While mentoring programs often focus on the importance of trusting relationships, these differences in the bases of trust are rarely acknowledged and discussed. I hope this explanation has made you aware of how you can avoid missteps—especially in a cross-gender mentoring relationship.

Pitfall # 4: Lack of Focus on Business Acumen

While mentoring programs offer ample advice about forming trusting relationships, they offer scant advice about the importance of developing business acumen. As I've suggested before this is, perhaps, the most serious problem with today's formal mentoring programs.

Our research indicates that when it comes to identifying and selecting candidates with high potential (HIPO in the chart below), 50% of the criteria for selection have to do with business, strategic and financial acumen! Very few organizations proportionately weight The Missing 33% (O)—business, strategic and financial acumen.

As you see in the chart below, they either over-emphasize competencies that have to do with personal greatness (P) or with skills for engaging others (E). For example, companies A–G are all Fortune 500 companies. None of them comes close to the 50% weight on outcomes that our research discovered is sought in high potential (HIPO) candidates. The same is true for a well-known competency deck, 360° assessment and the open enrollment programs offered by an international management training company.

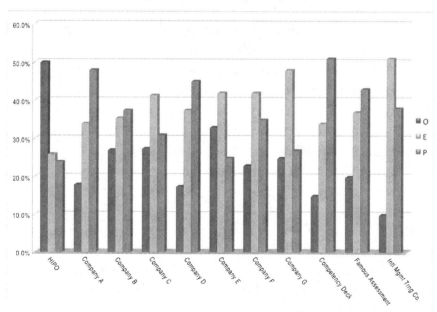

Very few leadership models (or leadership training programs) come anywhere near that weighting. This is one of the reasons why mentoring advice, discussions and experiences rarely focus on what the protégé can do to grow business, strategic and financial acumen.

Pitfall # 5: Promise of Advancement

Best intentions aside (and for good reasons), many mentoring programs were originally designed to help women and other underrepresented groups advance. That's why, when high potential employees are chosen to participate in a formal mentoring program, the message can inadvertently be that participation comes with the promise of advancement. This can create a sense of personal entitlement in the protégés and place an unfair burden on the mentors. It also created backlash from men who felt excluded.

Organizations have countered this pitfall by disconnecting participation in formal programs from the expectation of advancement and by making the programs open to anyone. This watering down of the goals isn't a real solution.

Pitfall # 6: Watered-Down Expectations

By disconnecting mentoring from advancement, companies lose sight of the fact that men were mentored as an informal strategy for creating a pipeline of talent that could make greater contributions to the business. By serving everyone and by moving to online matching, mentoring programs as a tool for grooming talent are diminished. As a matter of fact, some are now dubbed "structured social learning" or "open learning."

A recent report[4] stated that participants rated "expanding my network," "interpersonal effectiveness" and "confidence in role" as the top three areas they improved as a result of open learning. Notice, not a word about enhanced business, strategic or financial acumen. Nothing said about understanding how the organization works or how decisions are made at higher levels. No report of increased readiness to contribute in a larger role.

Women also have diminished expectations. The advice of many programs is rooted in a time when as "outsiders" women were advised to find a trusted confidante who could help them figure out how to gain the confidence and knowledge required to build a career. Not much has changed. Today, women expect mentoring to offer[5]:

- Advice and feedback on how to improve.
- Emotional support.
- Increased sense of confidence and self-worth.
- Focus on personal and professional development.
- Insight into themselves, their styles and what may need to change.
- A personal connection.
- Caring, altruistic advice.

When women enter mentoring relationships expecting benefits such as these, we are expecting too little...and not the right things.

It's not enough that corporate mentoring programs enable women and men to enter mentoring relationships. They must produce greater benefits—to the mentors, protégés and organization. By avoiding these 6 pitfalls, you will fulfill the expectation that mentoring programs will help women advance.

New Expectations for Mentoring

So let's recap what we know. First, conventional wisdom about mentoring ignores The Missing 33%. Therefore, women are not being mentored in the one area they most need in order to advance to the ranks of senior leadership. Second, because of several pitfalls, corporate mentoring programs are not fulfilling their potential for supporting women's advancement.

So what should women expect from mentoring and what should mentoring programs offer? Here are my suggestions on how we need to rethink mentoring.

First, let me propose a new focus for mentoring: Mentoring is the process by which employees are guided by more senior and/or experienced employees on:

- What's required of leadership and how to lead at different levels,
- A deeper understanding of the business of the business,
- Knowledge about what it takes to contribute to the business at higher levels,
- The formation of relationships that are strategic in nature and
- How to best leverage one's strengths in service of organizational goals.

Second, to be successful, corporate mentoring programs must:

- Require executives to commit to mentoring across differences, e.g., in gender, race or nationality.
- Require that these mentors choose protégés whose potential they believe in or on the basis of recommendations from respected colleagues.
- Focus heavily on the business and leadership knowledge protégés need in order to contribute to the organization (in other words, The Missing 33%).

These new expectations will contribute to women's clearer career goals, higher satisfaction, higher contributions and, potentially, advancement and retention. They also position the mentor to expend social capital to advocate for protégés who rise to the expectations for greater business and leadership savvy. And by fulfilling these expectations, mentors themselves hone the knowledge needed to be outstanding corporate citizens.

You might feel a bit challenged by these suggestions. If so, please ask yourself these questions. Are you uncomfortable with these expectations because:

1. They're inconvenient—for example because they aren't supported by the vendor who supplies your online mentoring software?
2. You think it's elitist to think that you should focus on senior/junior partnerships rather than peer-to-peer mentoring for example?
3. You are fearful of the reaction if you require executives to mentor across differences?
4. You hold the belief that mentoring is about being nurtured by a trusted confidante?

If you answered yes to any of them, I hope you'll take this opportunity to rethink mentoring.

If the mentoring program in your organization doesn't meet these new expectations and/or suffers from at least one of the 6 pitfalls, if not all, what's to be done? First, discover how mentoring programs and mentoring relationships can be improved. Second, take action to improve them. You can do this as a mentor, a protégé or as someone in charge of a mentoring program.

How? Read ON!

PART TWO

CAKE and PIE

Two Approaches to Mentoring

"Women have also been hesitant to give special treatment to other women for fear of being seen as Someone Who Favors Women. Singling out one individual for special attention can fly in the face of our image of ourselves as fair, objective people who don't play favorites. But the guys mentor young men all the time. We all know who the boss's favorite is, and that he'll do anything he can for him. In fact, it's considered somewhat unusual if the boss doesn't have a protégé."

—GAIL EVANS, AUTHOR SHE WINS, YOU WIN
CNN'S FIRST WOMAN EXECUTIVE AND FORMER WHITE HOUSE AIDE

CAKE Mentoring

At Leading Women, we've asked hundreds of women to tell us about the benefits they derived from their mentoring relationships. Here's what they tell us. Are any of these familiar to you?

"She gave me confidence."

"He pointed out areas that I needed to develop and strengths that were important."

"She was always there to give advice on how to handle a difficult situation or to coach me through figuring it out."

"He suggested that I get my Master's."

"She made sure that I knew what departments to connect with to get my work done and what processes I had to follow."

"He encouraged me to go after a job I never would have considered."

In part, these benefits describe the guidance outsiders need in order to be pioneers. They focus on boosting confidence, illuminating the path and pointing to opportunities that trail-blazers needed because

they didn't "know the ropes." And today, decades after women pio-
neered their way into corporations, many mentor/protégé programs
are still built to deliver benefits such as these. I group them into 4
categories and call this CAKE mentoring:

- **C**onfidence,
- **A**ptitude/Attitude/Advice,
- **K**onnection to resources and
- **E**ncouragement.

Confidence

Here's a question that will help explain why *Confidence* is such a big
part of CAKE mentoring. If you consider applying for a posted job
that catches your eye, what percent of the listed job requirements do
you feel you have to meet before you'd go ahead and apply?

If you're like the women in a recent study at Hewlett Packard, you
think you'd have to meet 100% of the requirements. If you're like the
men, you think you only need to meet 60% of the job requirements.

What this has to do with mentoring is this—for many men, gaining
confidence is NOT part of the recipe for career success, but for many
women it is. We often speak of mentors who help us gain confidence.
For example, Mary Sammons, former CEO of RiteAid, says about
her mentor, *"He believed in me and challenged me."*

And many women speak about building confidence as part of their
role as a mentor. Take for example Madeleine Albright who wrote in
her autobiography *(Madam Secretary):*

> *"People sometimes ask me how I want to be remembered…
> Perhaps some will…say that I helped teach a generation of
> older women how to stand tall and young women not to be
> afraid to interrupt."*

Researchers at Columbia Business School recently confirmed what
the H-P survey demonstrated: that men are more confident than

women.[6] As professor Ernesto Reuben says, men *"honestly believe their performance is 30 percent better than it really is."*

Until decision-makers learn to look past the appearance of confidence and possible overestimations of self-described performance to examine actual performance, many of us will have to build our confidence and become more skilled at self-promoting with grace and authenticity.

Aptitude, Attitude and Advice

Used here, *Aptitude* refers to how a mentor identifies the protégé's skills or points out her areas for development. As we know, performing from our platform of strengths is a key success factor.

At the same time, a mentor with a broader perspective often is able to see and point out latent aptitude or areas for development that the protégé could work on. Sharing these with the protégé helps her along her career path.

Charles Holliday, former CEO of DuPont, spotted Ellen J. Kullman as a potential successor in the early 1990s when they met in Tokyo. He ran Asia-Pacific operations and she was a visiting manager from the electronic imaging unit. One aptitude that caught his eye was Ellen's willingness to learn. *"There goes a future leader,"* Holliday is quoted as having thought to himself.

He also helped Ellen address a development area. He encouraged her to work with a coach to modify her impatient nature. Here's what she says about why this was important to her. *"If I made a statement before* [becoming CEO], *I was just one of the group. Now it's the law. I have to make sure I'm getting everyone's input."*

Early in her career, Christina Gold (former CEO of Western Union) worked at Avon. Mun Lavigne, the head of HR at the time, saw her potential and became her mentor. *"I read her performance appraisals,"* Lavigne told Claudia H. Deutsch of the *New York Times*, *"and I knew this woman should be moved ahead."* One of the ways he helped her develop her aptitude was to help her overcome her fear of public speaking. He required her to give a speech to senior management in New York and made her rehearse it repeatedly.

Many women receive "*Attitude* adjustments" from a mentor who acts as a confidante. They speak of the value of having a more-experienced advisor to help resolve problems with work or with people at work.

It can also describe the times when a protégé uses the mentoring relationship to unload or complain about her boss, the company and her work. As you've read, this is a use to avoid!

Advice, used as an element of CAKE mentoring, refers to how women use their mentor to discuss the challenges of being a woman at work, life balance issues, issues of harassment and/or discrimination.

Konnection to Resources

I know, I know, this isn't how you spell *connection*, but isn't CAKE a great acronym? *Konnection* refers to having someone put you in touch with the right people, right professional development opportunities, right internal resources for success, etc. Examples of konnection to resources include:

- Recommendations on courses and other resources that can help with career development.
- Invitations to attend a professional conference.
- Assistance attaining an important credential or degree.
- A broader perspective on connecting with the right people to access the resources (money, staff, knowledge, etc.) required for success on a current project/job (in other words the people who can teach you "the way we do things around here").
- Tips on job openings.
- Referral to a hiring manager.

As you've read, Ellen Kullman's mentor didn't just advise her to become more patient and inclusive...he *connected* her to a coach who would help!

Encouragement

In women's mentoring relationships *Encouragement* is often given or needed. For example, Carol Mullins, a *CIO* magazine "One to Watch," says that her mentors gave her *"the nudge that I sometimes needed to take a step I wasn't sure I could take."*

Nudges are required because women continue to blaze trails in so many professions, companies and industries. And, we often doubt our ability to take on bigger jobs, or believe that in order to take on a bigger job we must be ready to perform it from day one.

Recently a client mentioned that her CEO would like her to move into a line operations management position. Currently she is in a staff function, but the CEO obviously sees her potential for career growth. Like many women, she is hesitant about the move because she's not confident that she has the experience required so I passed on to her this wisdom from my recent conversation with Anne Mulcahy, former CEO of Xerox and current Chairman of the board of Save the Children.

When Anne first stepped into the CEO job at Xerox she was dubbed "The *Accidental* CEO." In spite of not having been fully prepared for the position she and her team successfully brought the company back from the brink of disaster. She advises:

> *"...no one comes into a job with all of the requisite knowledge and skills... I love to talk about the fact that this is doable. That nobody comes into this job (CEO) having all the tickets...* [asking for help] *actually builds your credibility versus detracts from it. It's amazing how much people love to be needed and to help."*

The point of Anne's message isn't that you have to aspire to become a CEO—she actually never did. It's that if the hardest job in a company—that of the CEO—is *doable* and *learnable*, so is the next job *you* could move into!

Sheryl Sandburg, COO of Facebook, has become a virtual mentor to women when she encourages us with this message:

> "...*do not leave before you leave. Do not lean back. Lean in. Put your foot on that gas pedal and keep it there until the day you have to make a decision....*"

We can see how important encouragement has been. Even those who've attained the highest levels speak about the importance of encouragement. As long as there are trails to blaze, CAKE mentoring is likely to remain an important element of women's career success.

A Tale of Two Protégés

My Story

When you think about your career can you identify a boss or someone else who gave you a boost? From early in my career, two people come to mind. I didn't know that they were *mentors* at the time, but a few years later—when discussions about mentoring began in earnest in corporate America—it became obvious to me that I benefitted from having been mentored by them. Let me introduce you to them because you might recognize yourself in my experiences.

My first corporate boss was Dave Chichester—a smart, visionary, personable and effective manager. He offered me two incredible opportunities.

The first was to be the user project manager on a key systems project to automate the payment of Long Term Disability Claims. When I was offered the project manager role, I had never seen a computer (yes, I'm *that* old!) and I didn't know what a Long Term Disability Claim was. Dave had allowed me to take a programming course that I dropped out of because I "just couldn't think that way." You can imagine my doubts about taking on the project, but he said to me, "You can do it."

The second opportunity was to head up the United Way campaign for the company. I can still remember the terror I felt at the kick-off meeting when I stood up to speak to hundreds of employees in the auditorium. But Dave's faith in my abilities helped me push through.

Both of these opportunities built my confidence, provided amazing leadership experiences and gave me great visibility. As did another initiative that had nothing to do with my job.

While working for Dave, I along with Priscilla Kania and Pat Minicucci launched one of the first corporate women's initiatives in the country. The stories about that are for another time, but that experience accounted for the fact that a woman named Wendy Susco knew who I was.

One day, about a year after completing the Long Term Disability project, my phone rang.

"Susan Colantuono," I answered.

The voice on the other end of the line said, *"Hi Susan. This is Wendy Susco."*

I'm thinking to myself, "Why's Wendy Susco calling me?" I knew that Wendy was the first and only woman attorney at my company— and probably within the entire insurance industry in Hartford at the time, but we had never met.

"Susan, there's a job open that I think you should apply for."

"What job?"

"It's a job in the training department that will involve facilitating workshops on issues of gender and race."

"Sounds interesting. Thanks, Wendy. I'll look into it."

I'm sure we talked a bit longer, but that's what I remember about our conversation.

Because our women's initiative had created an open job posting system, I was able to "look into" the job she spoke about. I applied for and got it. It was the job that set me on the path to where I am today.

Looking back I realize that Dave gave me confidence to tackle the big assignments he offered. And Wendy encouraged me to apply for a job that I never would have considered.

Along the way other mentors helped me learn and master my profession by giving me feedback about my strengths and areas for development, by being confidantes with whom I could discuss difficult situations and by guiding me to professional development experiences I should have.

I hope you recognize that for years I had a plenty of CAKE mentoring and that it made a huge difference in my career. But it wasn't until I met George Vecchione that I realized that CAKE was only half the recipe for mentoring success.

George Vecchione's Story

Decades after Wendy Susco's call put me on my career path, I was the architect of Lifespan's Center for Leadership Excellence. I invited George Vecchione, CEO of Lifespan (a system of hospitals in Rhode Island), to speak to senior managers in the Leadership Mastery program. Boy, were my eyes opened when I heard George's mentoring story.

As a young man working with a CPA firm, one of George's early assignments was a Medicare audit for Mount Sinai Hospital. He found the hospital intriguing, its mission compelling and its culture quite different from other businesses. And the attraction was mutual! Within 2 years the CFO hired him away from the accounting firm and into Mount Sinai's finance department.

Shortly after they met, the CEO of Mount Sinai, David Pomrinse, said to George, *"Make yourself available to attend meetings at my invitation."* As George came to find out, these meetings went beyond any that he would normally attend—they included executive team and board meetings.

George not only attended them as a passive observer, but ½ hour before a meeting David would sit down with him and pre-brief the meeting. He'd discuss the topic of the meeting, the participants and why each was there, what he (David) would be looking for and what he expected of each person. After the meeting he'd debrief it with George. They'd analyze dynamics such as: Who in the room had the power and why? Who made a credible argument and what made it credible? What decision prevailed and why?

When he attended board meetings, George describes his experiences this way:

> *"For the first months, I carried reports into the meetings and sat and listened. Then I was asked to present financial*

*information. The board members included CEOs and Wall
Street titans. They asked questions that I couldn't answer.
One focused heavily on cash. Another on revenue. It was
discouraging."*

After the meeting Dave supported him saying, "George, they like
you. They're just busting your chops." Bolstered by this reassurance,
George used the experience to hone his business and strategic acumen.

*"At first I guessed what they would ask. Then I began to
understand why they were asking. And then I started antici-
pating their questions and preparing my answers. I got so I
hit 9 out of 10."*

George also describes an important mentoring experience offered
by his boss, the CFO. George had been at Mount Sinai for a year
when the CFO became ill the night before a scheduled major presentation on Medicare to a prestigious regional healthcare forum.
Because George had helped prepare the material, the CFO asked
him to step in. George's success created a turning point in terms
of professional networks. Before the speech, George sought out
professional associations to be involved in. After the speech, they
sought him. He was an American Hospital Association delegate to
Washington at 30 years old.

At 29, George was recruited by New Rochelle Hospital to be its
acting CEO. While the search for a new CEO was underway, the
tragic Valentine's Day Massacre occurred—5 people were murdered
and many of the injured were brought to his hospital placing George
in the national spotlight. His calm handling of the catastrophe so
impressed the board, they called off the CEO search and offered
George the position.

As CEO, responsibility for setting and executing hospital strategy
rested in George's hands. Though no longer at Mount Sinai, George
continued to have Dave as a virtual mentor. Because Dave had taught

George about strategy setting and execution, George could ask himself, "What would Dave do?" He says,

> *"Asking what this more experienced executive would do was almost like sports. If you play against better competition, you play better."*

George acknowledges that Dave was very important to his career, but his story isn't built around gratitude for confidence, or encouragement. He tells it differently:

> *"Dave's mentoring allowed me to view things through more experienced eyes. It steered my perspective in the right direction."*

Do you notice the difference between the kind of mentoring George received and the kind I received? While he certainly received some CAKE mentoring, George was mentored primarily in the areas of strategy, business acumen and executive presence. By focusing on what George was mentored on, we understand why we have to shift our thinking about what mentoring is. We need to use mentoring relationships to get more of what I call PIE mentoring.

So what is your story? What kind of mentoring have you received? I hope you'll be thrilled when I tell you that a new recipe for successful mentoring means that if you've already been served a piece of CAKE, you *also* need a slice of PIE!

PIE Mentoring

Georges's story demonstrates that it's with PIE mentoring that men have been groomed. Here's how it happens. PIE stands for:
- Performance,
- Image, and
- Exposure

As best I can find, the acronym seems to have arisen (pun intended) and was originally coined by John Hammit, a Pillsbury executive.

You might be thinking, *"performance, image, exposure; DUH!"* but let me suggest that what those words conjure up in your mind might be different from what they conjure in the minds of men and women who mentor on them.

Performance

When you read the word *Performance* in the context PIE, you might think that *performance* means on-the-job performance—doing a good job. But, as George's story illustrates, **performance in the context of PIE means learning about the *performance of the business*—**how the organization works, the key outcomes that are indicators of its success and how what you do supports the key outcomes that executives are striving to deliver and boards are expecting.

In a mentoring relationship, *Performance* means using the mentoring relationship to learn (and speak) the business of your business.

In other words, filling in The Missing 33%—business, strategic and financial acumen.

During a workshop on The Missing 33% that I presented to women at MITRE Corporation, George Providakes, Chief Engineer, Command and Control Center, made a telling comment. He said:

> *"It's hard to imagine men being groomed and NOT being exposed to business acumen—as you get further up the organization, it consumes a proportionally larger part of your time. The discussions at the officer and director level are related to the business—how does the business go forward, how does the business evolve, where should the business be heading. If you were listening to* [our executive's] *presentation you would have observed that 99% of the discussion in his hour-long presentation was on strategy and outcomes.*

> *…We don't do a lot of training* [on business skills]. *Here we expect people to learn them by doing and through mentoring, not through training."*

Not only do organizations often do a poor job of emphasizing The Missing 33%, women receive far too little informal career advice about the importance of business, strategic and financial acumen. We asked 2000 women, "What is the best career advice you've received?" Only about **2% of women report that they have received advice about the importance of understanding and advancing the business of business.**

Image

When you read the word *Image*, you might automatically think of the modern-day equivalent of dress for success—right clothes, shoes, accessories and grooming. What successful executives think of is cultivating a *leadership presence*. As George did, they observe and discuss what makes executive communication effective or ineffective. Others talk about mentors who help them stand outside themselves, observe their behaviors and reflect on whether they are behaving as leaders.

Image for this discussion has little to do with attire. **You can be impeccably turned out in a "dress for success" way, but act like a subordinate OR you can be dressed very casually and act like a leader** (think Steve Jobs or Bill Gates). *Image* has has much to do with non-verbal carriage, speaking the language of business and how you wield the power of your position—no matter your level.

For example, before becoming CEO of Xerox, Ursula Burns was mentored by then-CEO Anne Mulcahy. Anne gave Ursula feedback on not telegraphing her opinions through facial expressions or verbally; advice about not *"letting my big mouth drive the discussion"* as Ursula explains. After meetings Anne would tell her, *"Ursula, they could read your face. You have to be careful. Sometimes it's not appropriate."*

You can get advice on having a leadership image if you know what to ask for—and anyone, man or woman, can give it if they know what to look for! You'll find great guidance about this in Part III.

Exposure

To round out the elements of PIE mentoring, when you read the word *Exposure*, I'm afraid of what you might be thinking! But George's story teaches us about 3 things—most of which have to do with The Missing 33%.

- Getting exposed to how work is done and decisions are made at higher levels.
- Having the right job assignments to position you to contribute at higher levels.
- Gaining exposure to people who can make a difference to your success.

Let's examine them one at a time.

Work at Higher Levels

George's experiences attending executive and board meetings are an excellent illustration of exposure to work at higher levels.

Not only did he get to meet the senior executives and directors, he was also **exposed to how work was done and decisions were made at higher levels.**

For example, George and the CEO would debrief each meeting discussing questions like:

- Why was this a topic on the agenda?
- What rationale carried the most weight in making the decision?
- How will the decision affect the hospital?

Remember what George said about working with Dave: *"Dave's mentoring allowed me to view things through more experienced eyes. It steered my perspective in the right direction."* He ultimately used that perspective to think through what the board might ask him. In other words these experiences helped George learn how to think like a CEO *and* like a director, both of which prepared him to step into the CEO role at a young age.

The Right Opportunities

Interviewing a key executive of a Fortune 50 company gave me insight into how he thought about the relationship between career success and exposure to key assignments. He described a 4-box model by which he categorizes talent. He looks for *A players* in *A positions.*

A players are those with a great track record of advancing business outcomes, who are easy to work with and have demonstrated leadership talent.

A positions are close to operations—where it's easy to learn about the business of the business and make an impact on business outcomes. These are the "right opportunities" to reach for.

Being an *A player* in an *A position* places you in the top right-hand quadrant of the diagram on the next page. This is where executives look to identify high potential (Hi-Po) talent.

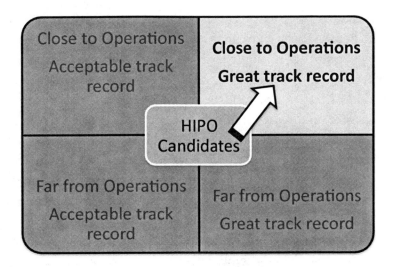

Women often don't understand the importance of *A positions* to career success, but several of the Fortune 500 women CEOs did.

Christina Gold, former CEO of Western Union, took a step down at one point in her career to gain the management experience she needed to move up later.

Early in her career, Brenda Barnes, former CEO of Sara Lee, was VP of marketing for Frito-Lay (a Pepsi company). With an eye to her future advancement, her mentor at the time suggested she leave marketing (a staff function) and move into sales (an *A function*). She did this when she left Frito-Lay to go to PepsiUSA.

The most important *A positions* are running business units. It's noteworthy that at some point in their careers, nearly all of the Fortune 500 women CEOs ran businesses and had direct responsibility for their financial success.

People Who Make a Difference

Ultimately, George began making presentations to the board. He leaned into the opportunity to present at the industry conference and to take the national stage during the Valentine's Day

Massacre. These experiences gave him the exposure he needed to become a serious candidate for the CEO slot.

Again, it's not only men who are given these experiences. Andrea Jung is the former CEO of Avon. She caught the attention of James Preston (then CEO of Avon who became her mentor) when as a relatively new hire she unified a number of geographic brands into strong global lines, oversaw total package redesign and brought on a new ad agency. As her mentor he gave her opportunities to speak at board meetings and increased her exposure to senior management. These experiences helped propel her into the top spot at Avon.

Remember Ellen Kullman, CEO of DuPont? No only did her mentor, Charles Holliday, help her develop a more inclusive and patient skill set, he also helped her join the General Motors board to broaden her executive perspective.

PIE mentoring goes a long way in addressing the flaws of formal mentoring programs because PIE mentoring—much more than CAKE mentoring—positions you to contribute to the organization and potentially *earn* sponsorship for career advancement. **That's why, whether you have one mentor or several, be sure that you get yourself a big slice of PIE!**

CAKE and/or PIE

Not long after I began to suggest that women most often get a piece of CAKE in their mentoring relationships when what they need is more PIE, I read a report from CareerWomen.com that reinforced this message.[7] They asked a number of protégés what types of assistance they received from their mentors. Whether they were men or women, here's what the protégés said about their women mentors.

Women mentors were most often acknowledged for offering informal fellowship and advice about navigating the organization as a woman. Women were also valued as mentors for offering gender-specific advice on work/life balance, flexible work arrangements, maternity leave, overcoming gender bias or dealing with gender dynamics and style advice that men might not address as effectively.

Women mentors were least likely to offer general business training (5%) and leadership opportunities (8%).

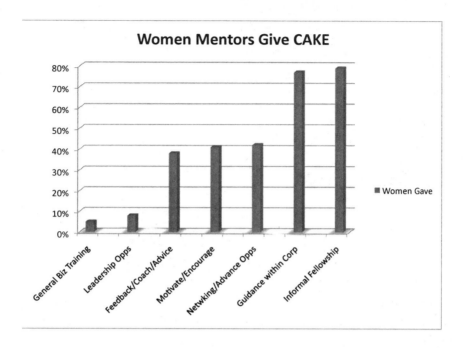

Women Mentors Give CAKE

This is not to say that women are only able to give CAKE mentoring. (There are many who serve up a slice of PIE as well—as you'll learn in the next section). And there's no doubt that having a piece of CAKE is a real treat. But CAKE mentoring totally ignores The Missing 33%. That's one reason why "let them eat CAKE" works as poorly for women protégés as for French peasants.

What did CareerWomen.com discover about the type of mentoring that men tend to give? Although they didn't use the term, they discovered that it's common for men to serve up PIE mentoring.

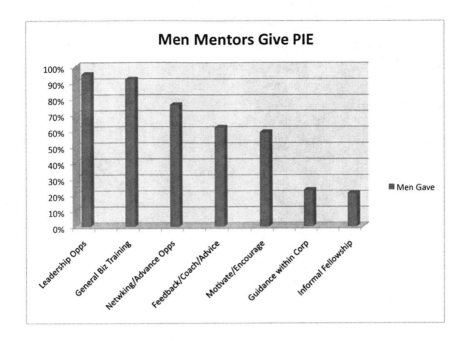

Over 90% of the time men were reported as providing *performance*-related mentoring: leadership opportunities and general business training. In this way, they proactively address The Missing 33%.

When George Providakes, Chief Engineer at MITRE Corporation, saw this data he said,

> *"I think what you're seeing is a prioritization of the value proposition of men versus women—people mentor on what they value...and these* [leadership opportunities and general business training] *are the priorities that men reflect..."*

When you look at the Career Women research side-by-side, you'll see that patterns of mentoring by women and men are exceedingly different. Men serve slices of PIE mentoring and women pieces of CAKE. I can't stress enough that this research doesn't mean that only men give PIE mentoring or that women only give CAKE. It simply means that at the time of the study, protégés reported that men are more likely to give PIE and women to give CAKE. As with any study, this describes group patterns and doesn't predict an individual's behavior.

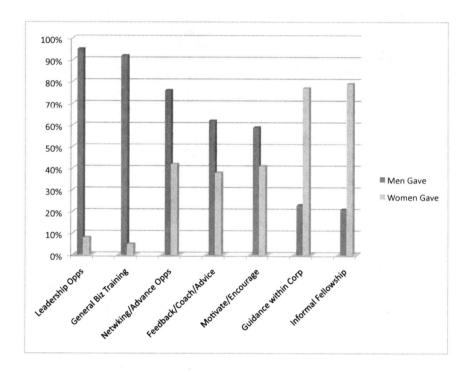

CAKE mentoring gives women the nudge they often need to succeed. But when it comes to preparing women to contribute at higher levels in the organization, they must have PIE mentoring!

Now, don't misunderstand me. I'm not saying that if you're a woman, you can only give CAKE mentoring. Obviously, the more you understand PIE mentoring, the easier it is for you to serve up a slice of it—and to make the most of time you invest in a mentoring relationship. That's just what we help you do in Part III.

Nor am I saying that if you want PIE mentoring you should have a man as a mentor. You can get PIE mentoring from either a woman or a man if you know how to ask for it. That's just what you'll discover in the Tips chapters.

▶ Take a minute to reflect on your mentoring experiences. Download our *CAKE/PIE Assessments*. We have one for mentors and one for protégés.

PART THREE

Make the Most of Mentoring

"...the best mentor relationships are based on really knowing the person in some mutual interest. So at work, the best way for me to develop people is to engage with them substantively on an issue."
—SHERYL SANDBERG, COO
FACEBOOK

Tips for Protégés

Now that you understand that the goal of mentoring is to serve the organization *and* that PIE mentoring is essential for women, here are tips to make you a "perfect" protégé.

Tip # 1: Make a commitment to the mentoring relationship. Here's the commitment I'd suggest you make.

> **Protégé Commitment:** I recognize that it is an honor and privilege to participate in this program *and* that it is an awesome responsibility. Because the mentoring program exists to serve the organization's needs for leadership, I commit to my mentor to develop the business, strategic and financial acumen I need to contribute to the organization at higher levels and in different functions and, therefore, more effectively in my current position. I also commit to my mentor to work on my personal greatness and enhance my interpersonal skills. I realize that fundamentally the organization's mentoring program is not about me and that there are no guarantees that my participation will result in a promotion. My participation is about testing my potential to contribute. My participation is about proving myself worthy of my mentor's advocacy. And perhaps most importantly, my participation is about

being worthy of entering a pool of leaders prepared to contribute at higher levels.

Tip # 2: Invite Your Mentor to Read This Book. This will help align your expectations and provide you both with important tools and tips for your mentoring experience.

Tip # 3: Read *No Ceiling, No Walls* if you're truly interested in career success. Your career advancement rests on the foundation of your perceived leadership skills—no matter your level! Actually, enhancing your leadership skills is probably the most important goal for a mentoring relationship—and for women, conventional wisdom about leadership isn't sufficient. *NoCeilingNoWalls.com*

Tip # 4: Seek internal *and* external mentors. Mentors within and outside your organization offer different insights.

Internal Mentors
- Can help navigate specific political and cultural terrain.
- Know the landscape of internal opportunities.
- Help manage exposure by floating your name for internal projects and opportunities.
- Burnish your leadership brand.
- Can bring you along on his/her coattails.

External Mentors
- Offer career guidance from an outside perspective.
- Often have a broader perspective on the industry or profession.
- Can provide honest feedback with no on-the-job repercussions.
- Serve as a neutral sounding board with no vested interest in your current employment.
- Provide exposure to outside openings, conferences, speaking opportunities, etc.

Tip # 5: Focus on PIE Mentoring.
- Make sure that you spend a substantial amount of your mentoring time learning business, strategic and financial acumen and understanding business performance.
- Make sure that your mentoring relationship includes opportunities for feedback on and enhancement of your leadership image. Don't confuse this with personal branding. Your personal brand, professional brand and leadership brand (or leadership image) are distinctly different—although related. You'll find more information about this in the FREE Resources section.
- One of the things to learn through your mentoring relationships is what it takes to be an *A player* in an *A position*—in other words to place yourself in the upper right-hand quadrant of this model.

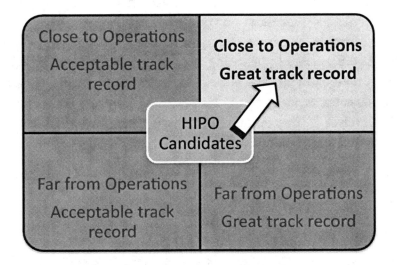

- Make sure that your mentoring relationship includes opportunities for understanding how decisions are made at higher levels and in different parts of the organization.
- Take opportunities to hear your mentor's perspective on job assignments that are offered to you.

- Discuss opportunities to gain exposure to key individuals.

Tip # 6: If your mentor doesn't offer you a "slice" of PIE, ask for it. Chances are good that you've never thought about asking for PIE mentoring and you might not know where to start.

Our *10 Questions Guide for Making the Most of Mentoring* will help. It contains 40 PIE-related questions: 10 for your internal mentor, 10 for an external mentor, 10 for getting mentoring on Image and Exposure and 10 for turning a project assignment into a mentoring opportunity. You'll find more information about this in the FREE Resources section.

Also, be sure to read the next chapter, even though it's written for mentors.

Tip # 7: PIE comes in different flavors depending on your level. As I discuss in *No Ceiling, No Walls,* leadership differs by level. What that means for PIE mentoring is that you need different skills, knowledge and experiences depending on your level.

For example, at career-start you first learn about your organization's *performance* by learning how your job fits into the whole. At mid-management, you should be listening to earnings calls to understand the strategy of the business and how you contribute. At senior levels, it's time to gain *exposure* to executives, the board and key external stakeholders.

▶ This is explained in the free resource *PIE Mentoring @ Different Levels.*

Tip # 8: Understand your Positional Purpose. This is a statement that connects what you do every day with the large strategic outcomes that are important to your organization. For example, instead of saying "I'm in customer service," you would say, "I reduce customer acquisition expenses by delivering outstanding customer service."

Knowing your Positional Purpose ensures that you will focus on doing what's best for the position and the company, not what's best for you. And never complain to your mentor about the responsibilities of your position.

Tip # 9: Focus on "what's in it for the organization?" Being a protégé is a profound responsibility. Instead of entering into a mentoring relationship thinking, "what can mentoring do for me," smart protégés think about the mentoring relationship as preparation for contributions to the organization at a higher level. A subtle, but important distinction. Ask yourself, "What skills, knowledge and experiences do I need to learn from my current position as I prepare to contribute at higher levels in the organization?" THIS is radically different from the mindset many protégés take into the relationship.

Tip # 10: Set clear goals. Know what you want from your mentoring relationship. Your most important goal will be to deepen or extend your leadership skills (enhanced skills in the areas of leading for outcomes, engaging and aligning others and personal leadership excellence). But you might also have goals for:

- Career navigation, e.g., what it takes to get to a specific level, into an *A position* or into a different profession.
- Specific knowledge or technical development, e.g., project management or financial acumen.
- Certain important experiences, e.g., insight into the perspectives of a different profession, how decisions are made at different levels or in different parts of the organization.
- Network extension, e.g., strengthening your internal and/or external strategic relationships.

Tip # 11: Be personable without being personal. If you're being mentored by a man, you don't want to be thought of as anything other than a competent businesswoman based on the topics of conversation you carry into the mentoring relationship. Some tips on being personable without being personal:

- Avoid conversations about self-doubt (as differentiated from discussions about skill development needs).
- Avoid conversations about personal family issues.
- For informal conversations consider talking about enjoyable vacations, the game you saw with your children last weekend, a great book you just read, the article about your company in the local/national news, etc.

Tip # 12: Know when to stop pushing back. Constant pushback breaks one of the cardinal laws of the Work World—as does public criticism. If you're having difficulty having your contrary opinions heard or living with a decision you disagree with, consider working with your mentor to:

- Strategize about the most effective way of voicing a disagreement...or to learn why what you said might not have been effective.
- Explore ways of presenting ideas so that you're seen as respectful even when disagreeing.

Once your boss has made a decision, never push back on it or publicly criticize it.

Tip # 13: Act with the utmost professionalism. Make only agreements you can keep, bring solutions for discussion—not problems to complain about—and disagree respectfully.

Tip # 14: Avoid the appearance of impropriety. Never meet your mentor for drinks in a romantic bar, beware of meeting behind closed doors or anything else that might give the appearance of impropriety. You don't want it to be said about you that "she slept her way to the top" and you don't want to compromise your mentor's reputation either!

Tip # 15: It's not about you! It is not your mentor's responsibility to help you advance; it is your mentor's responsibility to help you to learn the most about the organization that you can in your current position and prepare you to contribute at possible higher levels. To understand what this means, you have to understand what leadership looks like at every level. Again, this is a concept that is covered in *No Ceiling, No Walls.*

Tip # 16: Use mentoring throughout your career. Mentoring is a career-long activity. It's the flavor of mentoring that changes—especially the flavor of PIE! Here are two examples of how.

Denise Morrison, CEO of Campbell's, has said,

> *"I knew I wanted to be CEO...So I actually—literally... tracked everything I had done in every job and how long I stayed, what skills I built, how many people I managed ... and then I would circle the gaps.... When I found those gaps, I would say, 'Who could mentor me on that? Who could help me?'* **I'm still doing that to this day."**

As she has stepped into the CEO role, it's safe to say that she's receiving mentoring on working with her board of directors, Wall Street and other key external stakeholders (see #7 above).

Here's another example. Less than 2 years before she stepped into the CEO position at IBM, Ginni Rometty's boss connected her with a mentor to round out gaps in her development—among them extending her external strategic relationships.[8] (You might be interested to know that Ginni's mentor (Maggie Wilderotter, CEO of Frontier Communications) is the sister of Denise Campbell, CEO of Campbell Soup Company!)

Both illustrate that throughout your career and no matter how high your career takes you, there's always something to learn through mentoring.

Tip # 17: You have to earn sponsorship! In order to put his/her credibility on the line by backing you for a new opportunity, your mentor has to know that you have what it takes. You do this by demonstrating business, strategic and financial acumen (The Missing 33%) and proving yourself by delivering key outcomes—especially in *A positions*.

Tip # 18: Use CAKE Mentoring only as needed:
- Determine what confidence-building or self-promotion skill-building discussions or activities should be a part of your mentoring relationship.
- Frame your aptitude discussions around how leadership differs by levels and what it takes to succeed in other functions or on key projects. (Think of a career lattice, not simply a career ladder.)
- Beware of spending too much time on attitude/advice discussions—remember mentoring is about preparation to contribute at higher levels and/or in different parts of the organization.
- In your mentoring relationships make sure you're being "konnected" to important resources.
- Think about how encouragement is given or needed in your mentoring relationships.

Tip # 19: Keep your piece of CAKE small. At different points in your career CAKE will be more or less important. Early in your career, when you're in a new position and have to learn the ropes, when you're ready for a big next step or when you're considering a career transition—these are times when you might ask for a piece of CAKE.

Tip # 20: Minimize the use of A for Attitude adjustment. One of the attributes of successful people is the mindset of a "winner"—this means looking for solutions, not getting hung up on obstacles. Never complain! Always come to a mentoring discussion prepared with alternatives to talk over instead of a problem to be complained about.

Tip # 21: Start off on the right foot. You can build a collegial (personable) relationship by asking smart CAKE and PIE questions. Here are questions you can ask as you begin a relationship with a new mentor.

5 PIE Questions for the Start of Your Mentoring Relationship

1. **Performance:** Describe a turning point in your career when you understood what it meant to perform in service of organizational outcomes (instead of your own on-the-job performance).
2. **Performance:** How does your part of the organization deliver on key outcomes and organizational strategy?
3. **Performance:** What key metrics do you deliver and why do they matter?
4. **Image:** What advice have you received about cultivating a leadership image? Who gave it to you and why? How did you go about acting on it?
5. **Exposure:** What career move or special assignment has given you the clearest view into how our business operates?

4 CAKE Questions for the Start of Your Mentoring Relationship

1. **Confidence:** What important experiences were turning points in developing your sense of professional confidence?
2. **Aptitude:** When you were in my position (or at my level), what new skill was most important to develop and how did you get directed to develop it?
3. **Konnection to Resources:** What recommendations do you have about people I should talk with, courses or credentials I should go after, professional organizations to join, etc.?
4. **Encouragement:** If you hear of a position or other opportunity that would stretch me toward my goal, please let me know about it.

Tip # 22: Become a mentor. If you want to be a perfect protégé, you owe it to others to also agree to be a mentor. At Leading Women we call our mentoring program Be a Mentor/Find a Mentor. That's because we believe that everyone has something to teach and something to learn. To discover how to be a great mentor, read the next chapter.

Tip # 23: Read the chapter on Tips for Mentors. It will provide you with insights about the ways a mentor can support you.

Tip # 24: Buy your mentor a copy of this book. S/he might not know about the importance of PIE mentoring and this book will help explain it.

Tip # 25: Access our free resources. My final tip is to read the section on FREE Resources. There you'll find how to access all the resources mentioned above.

Tips for Mentors

You undoubtedly want to do an exceptional job as a mentor. At Leading Women we acknowledge this drive when we talk about *"master" mentors*. Now that you have shifted your perspective on the goal of mentoring *and* understand the importance of PIE mentoring you're better equipped to do your best as a mentor. Use the following tips to help you along the way.

Tip # 1: Clarify the nature of the mentoring relationship. Here's what I suggest you say to you protégé.

> **Mentor Statement:** "Because of what you already know about mentoring, you might think this program is about your career. If you do, you're seeing only part of the picture. There's an equally, or perhaps more important, reason for mentoring. I mentor to serve the organization. I mentor to ensure that the organization has top talent prepared to contribute at higher levels. I mentor to ensure that the organization has leaders to succeed the current leaders. I hope that you will make the most of this opportunity. I hope that you will prove worthy of the time I will invest in you. If you do, it could (there are no guarantees) make a difference in your career. If you don't, be assured that it won't."

Tip # 2: Invite your protégé to read this book before beginning the mentoring relationship. It will align her expectations with yours and provide her with valuable guidance, tips and tools to help her guide and get the most from the relationship.

Tip # 3: Remember that your protégé doesn't know what she doesn't know. You have a different and broader perspective than your protégé. While it's important for her to drive her learning goals, she doesn't know what you know about what it takes to succeed in your organization.

Chances are very good that conventional wisdom (and perhaps even your organization's competency model) is not helping your protégé accurately identify the gaps in her skills, knowledge and experience. This is something you're better positioned to do.

Tip # 4: Focus on leadership. If you're truly interested in supporting the success of your protégé, please take the time to read *No Ceiling, No Walls*. No matter her level, her ability to contribute to the organization rests on the foundation of her actual and perceived leadership skills. Actually, **helping her enhance her leadership skills is probably the most important contribution you can make**—and for women, much of conventional wisdom about leadership isn't sufficient.

Tip # 5: Abundantly offer PIE mentoring and offer CAKE mentoring judiciously and sparingly.

Tip # 6: Help your protégé learn about business Performance. You do this by helping her:
- Understand the business of your business and how she contributes to it.
- Hone her business, strategic and financial acumen (for example by discussing quarterly earnings reports or the annual report). One executive we know used the company's Yahoo! finance page to explain to his protégé the company's financial metrics, how they're derived and why they matter.

- Help her learn how to answer this question, "How would (specific person in a higher level or in another part of the organization) look at or handle this situation?" Ultimately, no matter her level, she needs to develop a perspective that will help her think like a CEO (or member of the board). As noted business guru Ram Charan writes in his book *Know-How:*

> *"It isn't necessary that you be a CEO to seek the big picture. While CEOs and business unit leaders need to see the external patterns to position the business, other leaders need this know-how, too, for instance, for HR to do talent planning, for operations to choose plant locations, and for R&D to find new sources of information."*

Tip # 7: Give guidance on your protégé's leadership Image. Make it a priority to give your protégé feedback on and opportunities to develop a strong leadership image both verbally and non-verbally.
- In her normal interactions with you.
- In meetings (live or virtual) where you observe her.
- When she gives a presentation (either live or taped).

Not sure what you need to look for? On our website you'll find a multimedia module on Executive Presence that will give you great ideas! You'll find more information on this in the FREE Resources section.

Tip # 8: Look for opportunities to help your protégé gain Exposure.
- Invite her to shadow you (e.g., at work, during outside board meetings, professional association meetings). Pre- and debrief the meeting/actions. (See #7 and 8 below.)
- Create other opportunities for her to attend meetings in different parts of the organization or of higher levels. They will broaden her perspective and help her understand how decisions are made in those different functions and higher levels.

- Help her identify the right professional and industry associations (or other external organizations) and the right roles to take in order to extend her network and build credibility.
- Invite her to professional, industry or other forums as participant and/or contributor.
- Recommend career moves (positions, parts of the organization, professional association membership/experiences) that will help position her to meet her goals. Pay particular attention to what are the *A positions* in your organization.
- Explain to her the ways you prepare presentations for people at higher levels. What perspective do they have? How do you tailor your content?

Tip # 9: When exposing your protégé to meetings or other events, pre-brief the experience. Pre-briefings help her look at a situation from your perspective (or that of your boss or other individual with a different perspective—perhaps from another function or an outside stakeholder). Discuss pre-brief questions such as:
- What makes this an important topic for discussion?
- What key outcome(s) are related to this?
- Which departments are likely to take what positions on the issue?
- Why is the attendee list comprised of those named?
- If you were making the decision, what would you decide and why?

Tip # 10: Debrief new experiences that you offer your protégé. Help her learn and cement key points. For example, if you let her shadow you at a meeting—ask debrief questions like:
- What did you learn about how decisions are made at this level or in our part of the organization?
- What was the most important discussion and why?

- What was the most important decision? Why was the decision made when other options were available?
- Who had power in influencing decisions? Why and how?
- Who made a good point, but wasn't listened to? Why?

▶ We've created a guide for protégés on PIE mentoring. It's a great resource for you, too. It's called *10 Questions Guide for Making the Most of Mentoring*. In it you'll find 40 PIE-related questions that can help you shape powerful discussions and experiences for your protégé.

Tip # 11: Keep your discussions focused on contributions at the next level or ways your protégé can use her current job to maximize learning about the organization. While you might occasionally be a sounding board as she works out how to best handle a particular challenge, set boundaries so you don't become a coach for performance issues in her current job—that's her boss's job.

▶ A resource that will help is our tool *PIE Mentoring @ Different Levels*. It explains elements of PIE mentoring that are important at different organizational levels. You'll find more information on this in the FREE Resources section.

Tip # 12: Support your protégé on her path—don't influence her to travel yours. Offer suggestions and advice, but leave the action commitments to your protégé (and expect her to follow through and report on progress). It's *her* responsibility to learn the most she can about how to make more substantive contributions to the organization.

Tip # 13: Mentor for development rather than for a specific position. In a recent workshop I delivered on mentoring, one of the participants kept claiming that to be an effective mentor he had to know his protégés desired position (meaning job title). This is not true. Your protégé might have no idea which positions she aspires to, but might be crystal clear about:
- Leadership skills to develop.

- Internal experiences to have (e.g., international assignment, strategic project, cross-functional team leadership, etc.)
- External experiences to have or networks to cultivate.
- Professional skills to enhance.

Clarity about any of these gives you fertile ground for cultivating a strong mentoring relationship.

Tip # 14: Encourage independence. Fight the urge to give your protégé the answers. Instead, invite her to think through options. This won't always work because sometimes you have insights she couldn't possibly have (see Tip # 2 above).

Tip # 15: Expect to learn from your protégé. One of the wonderful truths about mentoring is that mentors report learning as much from the experience as protégés. It's truly a reciprocal relationship. Her questions might point out areas that you need to learn more about—or show you how much you really do know. Her perspectives can open your eyes to a new way of seeing or doing. You can never predict what you will learn from a protégé, but you will always learn something.

Tip # 16: Start off on the right foot. You can build a collegial (personable) relationship by having smart CAKE and PIE discussions at the start of your relationship (see the CAKE and PIE questions at the end of the chapter on Tips for Protégés).

Tip # 17: Remember that the bases of trust differ by gender. If you're a man mentoring a woman, don't confuse humility or a discussion about her lack of confidence with lack of competence or ambition. And don't confuse a discussion about personal information with an invitation to intimacy.

Tip # 18: When necessary, build Confidence. You can help your protégé build confidence through:

- Providing positive feedback especially by highlighting her strengths.
- Helping her analyze the foundation of her successes to date.
- Offering stretch opportunities at which she can succeed.
- Pointing out the match between the protégé's experience/ skills and her goals, etc.
- Acknowledging, through your own experience, the fact that skill development is doable.

Tip # 19: Uncover Aptitude. Help your protégé identify her aptitude by working with her to take ownership of her current strengths, identify skills needed for future success, analyze the match between current strengths and needed future skills and discover any gaps.

Tip # 20: Offer guidance on Attitude adjustments (should be a minimal amount of time spent). These happen when you help your protégé examine a difficult situation through your different, more senior perspective.

Tip # 21: Konnect her to resources.
- Identify resources that your protégé needs for success, for example, programs to take, degree requirements, other credentials and when you make introductions to help facilitate these.
- Suggest books, websites, professional associations, industry associations, etc.
- Direct her to the correct processes and corporate resources to get something accomplished.
- Speak positively about your protégé to others in the organization.

Tip # 22: Offer Encouragement.
- Recommend that your protégé apply for a particular job, seek appointment to a special project, etc.

- Pass along information about an opportunity that would be beneficial for her and encourage her to go for it.

Tip # 23: Become a protégé if you aren't one already. Every leader at every level can benefit from a mentor. Being a protégé doesn't stop when you become CEO. In fact, that's often when you need a mentor the most. And, if you want to be an effective mentor for others, you also need to be a protégé. At Leading Women we call our mentoring program Be a Mentor/Find a Mentor. That's because we believe that everyone has something to teach and something to learn. To discover how to be a great protégé, read the previous chapter.

Tip # 24: Read the chapter on Tips for Protégés. It will help you understand what your protégé will be (or should be) doing and expecting.

Tip # 25: Buy your protégé a copy of *Make the Most of Mentoring*. If your protégé doesn't understand the importance of PIE mentoring or the important elements of a high-impact mentoring relationship, share this information with her.

Tip # 26: Access our free resources. Read the section on FREE Resources. There you'll learn how to access all the resources mentioned above.

Tips for Leaders of Corporate Mentoring Programs

Although it's not often calculated, time spent in mentoring relationships has a real cost in lost productivity. That's one of the reasons why your organization expects you to design a program that delivers a high return on the time invested.

Chances are that if you asked your executives to be honest about whether "expanding my network," "interpersonal effectiveness" and "confidence in role" are high-return benefits, they'd answer with a resounding "no."

On the other hand if you created a program with reported benefits such as "I use my network to advance key outcomes" or "I better engage others to hit key metrics" it would be highly valued. You can only get to those mentoring results if your program avoids the pitfalls we've discussed and adds a big slice of PIE!

Mentoring and Women's Advancement

I'm on record as an advocate for mentoring programs to support women's advancement. I've even coined the phrase ADVANCE Mentoring to call attention to the importance of PIE mentoring. This position developed before I fully understood the historic importance of mentoring as in informal succession planning tool.

Now that I know that the primary focus of mentoring should be to serve the needs of the organization for talent (as opposed to promising advancement for the protégé), I realize that advancement is the possible byproduct of mentoring relationships that address The Missing 33% and serve up a big slice of PIE.

And I'm all for women's advancement. Why? Because having women in executive management and on corporate boards is just plain good for business...and good for other women as well.

Does this surprise you? I hope not, but if it does, let's look first at the strong pattern of correlation between economic success and having a higher proportion of women at the top. Organizations as diverse as Catalyst (the global company specializing in research on women's advancement), McKinsey and the Glass Ceiling Research Center at Pepperdine have found a strong correlation between business performance and higher percentages of women at the top. These have ranged from 10% higher profit margin to 35% higher Total Return to Shareholders. In addition:

- In 2010, the World Economic Forum reported that "there is a statistical correlation between gender equality and the level of development of countries as measured by GDP and competitiveness." (One of their measures of gender equality is percentages of women in senior positions in organizations and on boards.)

- In July 2011 *USA Today* reported *"Fortune 500 companies that had a woman at the helm for all of 2009 were up an average 50%."* And according to *Forbes*, *"as a group they outperformed the overall market—companies dominated by male chief executives—by 28%, on average, and topped their respective industries by 15% [in 2010]."*

- NASDAQ.com reported the same about the period from January–November 2011. *"We've compared the performance of the current fortune 500 companies with women CEOs to the*

S&P500 performance and their industry competitors from the start of the calendar year to present. Correlation and causation aside, the trend holds true: women have been ruling the stock market."[9]

I don't believe that having women at the top necessarily *causes* higher performance. Rather, I believe that **women get to the top of high-performing organizations because of a virtuous cycle that values performance over patronage and competence over connections.** As a matter of fact, a *FORTUNE* article on companies with high percentages of women at the top characterized the companies as "fanatical about measurement, use empirical standards, clear goals and frequent reviews to identify and reward high performers."

It stands to reason that if the pipeline is full of women, companies that reward real performance will inevitably have more women at the top. Performance-focused companies (true meritocracies) are likely to achieve the higher performance described in these studies.

Now let's answer the question, why is it good for *women* to have other women at the top?

- Researchers at UNC Chapel Hill and UC Irvine found that companies with more women in senior management *increase pay equity from 77¢ on the man's dollar to 91¢.*[10]

- The Forum of Executive Women reports that at a "tipping point" of 3 women (or at least 25% on large boards), they begin to have a voice in governance.

  "It is often the women on boards who raise the most questions about how a company is cultivating a diverse pool of employees…"

  (At the time of their report, only 83 of the Fortune 500 companies had 3 or more women on their board.)

- The London Business School reports that at a critical mass of 30% women in senior positions, companies begin to *create cultures supportive of women's advancement.*

- Corporate Women Directors International reports in 2011 that companies with women CEOs have 22.3% women on their boards compared to 9.8% average representation of women on the boards of blue chip companies in the countries included in the study. This pattern holds in all regions no matter which country or what size company.

- Also from CWDI, women-led companies have a higher percentage of women in senior management at 24.3% than the average representation of women in executive roles in peer companies (12.2%). Again, while rates of increase may differ, this same pattern holds for the majority of companies with women at the helm in all regions of the world.[11]

Having women at the top creates a virtuous cycle that gets more women to the top. Having women on boards highlights the importance of running a company well enough that the best people are being promoted—regardless of race or gender. Having women in senior positions also cultivates cultures supportive of women's advancement—true meritocracies. And having women at the top increases pay equity.

And I'm all for using mentoring as one tool for filling the gaps in corporate talent development programs so that great talent rises to the top. If you agree and if your corporate mentoring program is designed to help elevate women, the following tips are immensely important—and they address each of the 6 pitfalls discussed in chapter 3.

Tips to Enhance Your Mentoring Program

Tip # 1: Retain high expectations. Don't settle for mentoring programs where the main benefits are:
- Advice and feedback on how to improve.
- Emotional support.
- Increased sense of confidence and self-worth.
- Focus on personal and professional development.

- Insight into themselves, their styles and what may need to change.
- A personal connection.
- Caring, altruistic advice.
- Expanded network.
- Interpersonal effectiveness.

Instead design a program where participants will say they benefitted because they:
- Better understand the business of their business.
- Can articulate how what they do drives key outcomes.
- Know how their actions support the overall strategy.
- Understand the story behind the financials.
- Can better cultivate strategic relationships inside and outside the organization and use them to advance the business.

Even though it may seem counterintuitive, when your program focuses on helping the protégé deliver benefits to the business and not on her career advancement—advancement is more likely to occur.

Tip # 2: Encourage PIE mentoring. Many corporate mentoring programs over-focus on the process and form of mentoring and under-focus on enhancing business, strategic and financial acumen—what we call The Missing 33%. That's why the abundant resources available through Leading Women's Be a Mentor/Find a Mentor program are primarily focused on PIE mentoring.

If your program's supporting resources ignore or under-focus on The Missing 33%, take action today to correct the deficit!

Tip # 3: Avoid forced matching. When companies are smart about matching mentors with protégés, the chances of success are far greater than if matches are made online or through human intervention.

Consider requiring your executives each of his direct reports to identify women to mentor.

For example, at Williams (an energy company), Rory Miller, president of the Midstream business, and Alison Anthony, director of diversity and community relations, launched a mentoring program. Rory required each of his direct reports to nominate women to become protégés. The chosen protégés are quite diverse in background and in level—from individual contributors to managers. And because the executives selected women in whom they had confidence and saw potential, the program is on its way to fulfilling its goals.

Tip # 4: Realize that a formal *sponsorship* program is not the solution. Catalyst, the research organization focused on expanding opportunities for women, suggests in a recent report that a mentor is different than a *sponsor* and that to advance women need sponsors (who will use influence to advocate on their behalf) more than mentors.[12]

But I believe the distinction between a mentor and sponsor is a false one. We already know that traditional definitions of mentoring include *sponsorship* and *support*. And in the 1970s the word *mentor* was synonymous with someone who advocated on behalf a protégé's career.

While it's true that earning an *informal* advocate is important, I worry that this distinction will continue to gain currency and result in the creation of *formal* sponsorship programs that won't work any better than formal mentoring programs have in the past.

If this research has caught your attention, please understand that creating a formal sponsorship program with the same attributes as past mentoring programs won't help advance women—it will encounter the same pitfalls.

Even NAFE's Top Companies for Executive Women recognize that sponsorship programs with forced matching don't work. Although AMEX has a program called "Pathways to Sponsorship" it forges pairs that *"could grow into sponsorship."* It's only a possibility that sponsorship will arise. Why? Because, as Kerrie Peraino, SVP of International HR and Global ER, points out, *"You can't ring me up and ask me to be your sponsor. I do that when I see your work and I advocate for it."*

As with Williams' mentoring program, DuPont has a *sponsorship* program that avoids the forced matching pitfall by gaining commitments from 6 executives with P&L responsibility for major platforms to commit to advancing 6 women each within 2 years. As at Williams, the executives choose the women they work with.

The key point here is that whether you call your program mentoring or sponsorship—be sure to avoid the forced matching and other pitfalls we explored earlier.

Tip # 5: Reduce the sense of protégé entitlement. A couple of years ago a client called me to talk over a problem she was having with the mentoring program at a large healthcare system. She said, *"We just completed our evaluation of the program. It ended about 6 months ago. While the protégés and mentors enjoyed the time they spent together; overall the protégés were dissatisfied."* When I asked her why, she said, *"All of the protégés expected that they would receive a promotion."*

Two factors contributed to their wildly unrealistic expectations.

- First, protégés were told that they had been chosen by their CEOs—a factor that contributed to their sense of entitlement. There's nothing wrong with this in and of itself. But coupled with this was a second factor.
- The expressed focus of the program was the development of the individual, not the demand for a greater contribution to the organization.

When you are using mentoring programs to help develop talent, the focus must remain on mentoring as a tool to garner stronger contributions to the organization, not to ensure advancement of the individual.

To get a sense of how to position or reposition your program, read the protégé and mentor commitments in the preceding Tips chapters.

Tip # 6: Get real about *"trusting relationships."* I cringe each time I read or hear the advice that a mentor and protégé must develop a trusting relationship. And while a certain level of trust is required in order to exchange feedback, this advice is unhelpful for 3 reasons. It is given:

- On the assumption that the relationship will be built on CAKE mentoring and all the warm, nurturing interchanges that connotes (i.e., emotional support, a personal connection, caring, altruistic advice).
- Without any guidance about gender differences in what trust means and how it is earned (e.g., being personable without being personal, having your mentor's back, respectful disagreement).
- Without the understanding that much of PIE mentoring requires a fairly low level of trust (i.e., you don't have to have a deep trusting relationship to discuss the business implications of a financial reports).

If you must counsel your mentors and protégés to develop trusting relationships, at least guide them toward an understanding of the gender differences discussed earlier and offer them the tips from the Tips for Protégés chapter.

Tip # 7: Access our free resources. Read the section on FREE Resources. There you'll learn how to access all the resources mentioned in previous chapters.

Tip # 8: Become a protégé and mentor. The best way to enhance your corporate mentoring program is to experience it yourself firsthand.

Mentoring Matters

I'm not only passionate about getting more women to the top of organizations and onto corporate boards; I'm also passionate about helping *you* create a career that soars. Now you know that getting mentored on the right things can make that happen for you.

The right kind of mentoring is important not just for *your* career success, it's important for women's collective career success. Even if another woman moves ahead of you on the corporate ladder, consider what Gail Evans has written in *She Wins, You Win:*

> *"There's only one rule that matters, one rule that I have not seen written about in any book, article or web site. That one rule is this: Every woman must always play on the women's team. Why? Because every time any woman succeeds in business, your chances of succeeding in business increase. And every time a woman fails in business, your chances of failure increase."*

I hope that you'll use mentoring to help create a career that soars, and at the same time be sure you're playing on the women's team. No matter your level, make sure that you're mentoring another woman! And be sure you're serving her a big slice of PIE.

Mentor ON!

Susan

Susan L. Colantuono
Wakefield, RI USA
and
La Louviere, France

P.S. I welcome your comments or questions. And, if you want to receive advance information on upcoming books in the ASK Leading Women series, e-mail me: *Susan.Colantuono@LeadingWomen.biz.*

FREE Resources

For Protégés, Mentors and Those Running Corporate Mentoring Programs

- **CAKE and PIE Assessment for Protégés**—Self-reflection activities to help protégés better understand how to structure mentoring.
  - Download at *www.MaketheMostofMentoring.com*

- **CAKE and PIE Assessment for Mentors**—Self-reflection activities to help mentors better understand how to structure the mentoring experience.
  - Download at *www.MaketheMostofMentoring.com*

- **PIE Mentoring @ Different Levels**—Provides mentors and protégés with examples of how PIE mentoring will differ depending on whether the protégé is an individual contributor, manager or executive.
  - Download at *www.MaketheMostofMentoring.com*

- **10 Questions Guide for Making the Most of Mentoring**—Contains 40 PIE-related questions: 10 for internal mentors, 10 for an external mentor, 10 for mentoring on Image and Exposure and 10 for turning a project assignment into a mentoring opportunity.

- E-mail us at *info@LeadingWomen.biz*

- **Executive Presence Module**—Multimedia module that explains the difference between personal and executive presence. It's an essential when the topic is enhancing the protégé's leadership Image.

  - View online at *www.MaketheMostofMentoring.com*

Be a Mentor/Find a Mentor

Leading Women offers a cross-company mentor match application. It's a FREE benefit for our **GOLD** and **PLATINUM Members.** If your organization doesn't have a mentoring program, this would be a great way for you to find a mentor. If it does, you can use our program to find a mentor in another company.

Be a Mentor/Find a Mentor is based on the premise that everyone has something to teach and everyone has something to learn. That's why in order to find a mentor, you have to sign up to be a mentor!

Our program also gives you access to over 8 articles, 3 guides, 8 worksheets, 2 videos and 3 Tip sheets that offer additional information and tools to help you make the most of your mentoring relationships. Based on the research covered here in *Make the Most of Mentoring*, these unique resources address all 6 phases of the mentoring relationship. They will help you:

- Identify your goals for the mentoring relationship.
- Choose your mentor.
- Introduce yourself to your mentor.
- Plan your initial meeting.
- And more.

While some of the content is specific to our Be a Mentor/Find a Mentor program, most of it will be important to you whether you are, or would like to be, in a mentoring relationship.

Become a **GOLD** or **PLATINUM Member** today to find an external mentor. Or **e-mail us** to discuss licensing our application to support your mentoring initiative: *info@LeadingWomen.biz.*

Create a Career That Soars!

Leading Women supports your success from career-start to the C-suite and onto corporate boards.

Live Leadership Programs

These inspiring, informative and engaging multi-session programs offer content specific to the demands of leaders @ every level. From our Ready, Set, LEAD™ program for emerging leaders to our Leadership Mastery™ program for senior managers, you'll find a program that is just what you need to power your success.

http://www.LeadingWomen.biz/Leadership

Leadership Excellence Assessment™ (LEA)

Wondering how people above you perceive your business, strategic and financial acumen (along with other key leadership skills)? Our unique LEA is for you. One Fortune 500 CEO has described this unique 360° assessment as, *"the most comprehensive assessment I've ever seen."* Learn more about it here:

http://LeadingWomen.biz/storelistitem.cfm?itemnumber=10

Virtual Leadership Solutions

Can't make it to our live programs? You can still support your career aspirations with the same unique and innovative content. Invest in a

PLATINUM Membership or Corporate Partnership to gain access to our online resources. These include teleseminars, multimedia self-paced modules, interviews with thought leaders, authors and executives and more.

http://www.LeadingWomen.biz/Join

Develop Top Talent

Overcome the common barriers to women's advancement with our uncommon solutions designed for diversity initiatives, learning and development functions and women's networks. Leading Women's live, online and Self-Managed Solutions™ provide the career-advancing skills and knowledge that women need.

Expand Your Talent Pipeline
It takes stellar strategies to develop top talent. You might not realize that means eliminating gender-related constrictions from your talent pipeline. Leading Women helps companies assess and eliminate gender-bias in four systems and develop long-term strategies for expanding your talent pipeline.

1. Management/Leadership/Career Development—identify constrictions due to disproportionate emphasis on developing interpersonal skills.
2. Performance Management—open your talent pipeline by ensuring that business, strategic and financial acumen skills are identified and measured as appropriate at all levels from individual contributor to senior manager.
3. High-Potential/Succession—ensure that your criteria for high potential designation and succession planning encourage women to meet rigorous business, strategic and financial criteria for advancement.

4. Mentoring Programs—help women expand beyond good
    relationships by using those relationships to develop
    business, strategic and financial acumen.

Contact us to discuss these and other areas essential to women's
advancement.

info@LeadingWomen.biz | +1-401-789-0441

Strengthen Your IWiN*

IWiNs often get a bad rap. A *BusinessWeek* article highlighted this problem when it reported that,

> *"Corporate women's networks frequently... toil on the fringes, hosting 'lunch and learns' and book clubs that rarely provide the skills or exposure women need to rise in the ranks...such initiatives are flourishing...Networks are cheap, usually relying on female volunteers...may become little more than social gatherings, and have trouble attracting heavy hitters."*

Leading Women transforms IWiNs from marginal to essential through these services.

IWiN Strategic Alignment
Whether you're starting an initiative or planning future activities, Leading Women helps ensure relevance, alignment with business goals and measurable positive results. Read about our clients' successes: *www.LeadingWomen.biz/Cases*.

---

* IWiN is our abbreviation for Internal Women's Initiative, Network, employee resource group, business resource group, affinity group, etc.

IWiN Leadership Development

Cultivate leadership skills, plan for succession and develop future IWiN leaders with Leading Women's Self-Managed Solutions™, IWiN newsletters and consultation.

To discover the many ways that Leading Women can help strengthen your IWiN, call for a free 30-minute consultation at +1-401-789-0441.

About the Author

When Susan Colantuono was 16 months old, her brother was born, thus launching a lifelong interest in gender dynamics and an abundance of heretical observations and breakthrough thinking. With a clarion call to action and practical advice Susan's nononsense and comprehensive insights guide women to more inspired and confident leadership... and more fulfilling careers.

Susan shares her wisdom as CEO of Leading Women, where she inspires and powers the success of women leaders in organizations and through her speeches and writings. Her book, *No Ceiling, No Walls: What women haven't been told about leadership from career-start to the corporate boardroom*, has been described as a "must read" by CEOs and thought leaders alike. It's used at organizations including AACE International, DePuy (a J&J company), Kodak, MassMutual, New York Life, PepsiCo, Professional Women in Healthcare, OfficeMax, Prudential, Sodexo, Sunoco, The MITRE Corporation and many others!

Susan is one of Rhode Island's two delegates to Vision 2020, is past director of the Rhode Island State Council of the Society for Human Resource Management (SHRM) and has been honored by *Providence Business News* as Ally and Mentor for Business Women.

She loves her family, the south of France, horse camping in Yellowstone and Lindt Excellence 85% Cocoa Bars...not necessarily in that order.

Endnotes

1   First known use of the word "mentee" was in 1965.
    http://www.merriam-webster.com/dictionary/mentee

2   *http://dictionary.reference.com/browse/mentor*

3   *The Male Factor* by Shanti Feldhahn

4   *http://www.astd.org/TD/TD_Jan11_CreatingNewMindset.htm*

5   *http://blog.globalnovations.com/index.php/talent-development/
    mentoring-and-sponsoring-women/*

6   *http://au.ibtimes.com/articles/259244/20111201/men-s-over
    confidence-propel-leadership-roles-firms.htm*

7   *http://www.prweb.com/releases/2003/07/prweb72296.htm*

8   *http://online.wsj.com/article/SB1000142405297020450530457700
    0222269670752.html*

9   *http://community.nasdaq.com/News/2011-11/girl-power-list-of-
    companies-with-female-ceos.aspx?storyid=101171*

10 *http://uci.academia.edu/MattHuffman/Papers/87577/Working_
    for_the_Woman_Female_Managers_and_the_Gender_Wage_Gap*

11 *http://www.globewomen.org/cwdi/cwdi_2011_Women%20CEOs
    %20Press%20Release.html*

12 *http://www.catalyst.org/publication/458/42/mentoring-necessary-
    but-insufficient-for-advancement*

CPSIA information can be obtained at www.ICGtesting.com
Printed in the USA
BVOW040124300712

296508BV00005B/8/P